GW00775799

Sky and Landscape

– IRENE EARIS –

An environmentally friendly book printed and bound in
England by www.printondemand-worldwide.com

Mixed Sources
Product group from well-managed
forests, and other controlled sources
www.fsc.org Cert no. TT-COC-002641
FSC © 1996 Forest Stewardship Council

PEFC Certified
This product is
from sustainably
managed forests
and controlled
sources
www.pefc.org
PEFC/16-33-415

This book is made entirely of chain-of-custody materials

i

www.fast-print.net/store.php

Sky and Landscape

Copyright © Irene Earis 2011

ISBN 978-1 78035-059-2

First published 2011 by
FASTPRINT PUBLISHING
Peterborough, England.

Sky and Landscape

A Field Guide to Archaeoastronomy

Irene Earis

illustrated by

John Bingham

Pictures of megalithic sites, whether modern
photographs or old engravings such as this one of
Stonehenge (above), almost always include the
sun or the moon. This book explains why.

Heartfelt thanks to:

John Bingham for his superb illustrations and work on layout and production, as well as being the ideal calm and enthusiastic co-worker throughout.
Kathryn Bingham for her warm support and expertise.

Robin Heath, good friend and model archaeoastronomer, for generously contributing so much of his time, research and advice.

Roger and Harriet Earis for all their loving help and support.

Tony Ropper for freely sharing the material on his website www.megalithicsites.co.uk

Subhashis Das for his work on the Rola alignment in India.
Victor Reijs for his work at the Treasury of Atreus.
Gordon R. Freeman for his work at "Canada's Stonehenge".
Dr.Euan MacKie for his work at Brainport Bay, Scotland.

And to our ancestors whose patience, ingenuity, hard work and vision have left us the opportunity to glimpse an understanding of a larger reality through the stone monuments they have left behind them.

Drawing of a sailing boat on pottery from Southern Egypt c.2900 BCE.
Navigation using the stars was an essential part of life in the ancient world

Contents

Visiting Prehistoric Sites

Asking the right question

People love to visit prehistoric sites such as stone circles, passage mounds and dolmens, amazed at their antiquity and the beauty of the stones. Some sites, such as Stonehenge in England or New Grange in Ireland are internationally famous and attract tourists in their thousands. Some are small, remote and hardly noticed. But a typical experience that visitors have, despite guide books and information boards, is to wander around without understanding the real purpose and significance of the site, while at the same time feeling that there must be an explanation somewhere that could help them.

This is what this book is about; not to present the "mysteries of the megaliths" but to offer some knowledge and a method of approach that will genuinely help to bring clarity and understanding to these megalithic sites and their builders.

The starting place is to ask,:

Why were these stones erected here and not somewhere else?

The location chosen is the biggest clue to understanding them. And the answer to the question lies almost always in the sky, especially on the horizons visible from the site, where the sun and/or moon can still be seen to rise and set close to their same positions thousands of years ago.

Certain days of the solar year and of the moon's much longer cycles were marked by aligning the stones to these horizon points. Place then also became a point in time where astronomy and aesthetics could be combined.

Examples of prehistoric structures with astronomical alignments

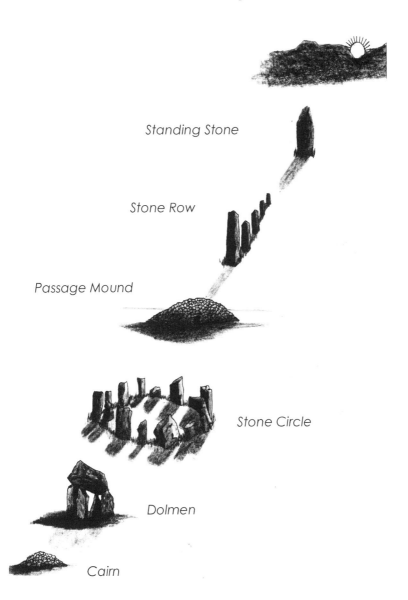

Standing Stone

Stone Row

Passage Mound

Stone Circle

Dolmen

Cairn

Archaeoastronomy

Don`t be afraid of all those vowels in the middle!

The word "archaeoastronomy" is formed by a combination of "archaeology" and "astronomy". Although the word looks difficult, however, the idea behind it is simple and obvious. Archaeoastronomy (or "astroarchaeology") is the study of the placing of structures of all kinds, prehistoric to modern, to align on particular days with the sun or moon on the horizon. Countless structures in the ancient world were astronomically aligned.

Even in the modern era churches were often built on an east/west line or orientated towards the sunrise of the festival day of the church`s patron saint. It is only in very recent times that human beings, with roofs over their heads and clocks to tell the time, have lost touch with the changing patterns of the sky.

In the past people spent far more time out of doors day and night all year round. Until about 1000 BCE the climate in temperate latitudes was warmer and the skies clearer. A glance up at the sun could indicate from its position the season of the year and how many hours of daylight were left. Equally a glance up at the sky at night could indicate the time by the revolving "clock" of the circumpolar stars and the stage of the month by the position and shape of the moon. Nowadays when we talk of "landscape" we hardly think of the sky at all, but in historical terms we are the odd ones out.

On the horizon the sun and moon look the same size (half a degree in width). The sun is 400 times larger than the moon, but curiously it is also 400 times further away from the earth.

What is an alignment?

An alignment usually consists of an observing location with some deliberately placed stone or structure (the backsight or nearsight), and a natural feature or another man-made item such as a cairn on the horizon (the foresight or farsight) where the sun or moon rise or set on a particular day.

The alignment can be more precise when the foresight is a long way off. Parc y Meirw in South Wales, for example, is a lunar alignment linking a row of large standing stones with the skyline ninety miles away across the sea in Ireland.

Above: at the mound of Torrylin on the island of Arran, Scotland, the south-facing chamber points directly at the island of Ailsa Craig on the horizon in the distance.

No one knows whether in prehistory people marked the sunrise and set when they saw the first flash, when half the orb sat on the horizon or when the whole orb was visible. There were probably local variations, but the first and last flashes are usually considered the easiest to see and mark. Otherwise the sun can be too dazzling to look at unless a cairn, slope or island half-blocks the light. Remember never to stare directly at the sun without protecting your eyes.

4

Some examples of the kind of horizon markers that a site might be aligned to:

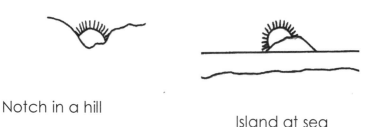

Notch in a hill

Island at sea

Cairn on a hill

Two hills forming a notch

Where land meets sea

A Scottish Landscape with Natural Horizon Markers

Professor Thom in this diagram from his book "Megalithic Sites in Britain" (1967) showed how distant peaks in Caithness, Scotland stand out against a smooth, nearer skyline, thus performing the same function as manmade cairns on the horizon.

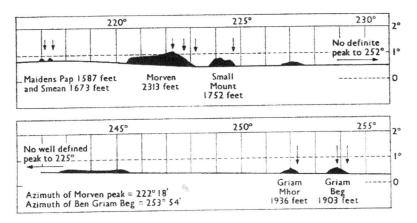

Horizon to south-west from stones near Watton, ND 223516. Arrows indicate measured points.

When walking in hilly landscapes, look out for the way distant peaks may suddenly emerge in the distance, protruding over closer smooth skylines. If the astronomy fitted, stones and cairns could be erected as backsights at these points without the necessity of building a foresight on the horizon.

Every landscape has unique potential for linking earth to sky and it is an entertaining exercise to watch the horizons as you walk and drive around the country in order to work out how you would utilise their distinctive profiles to link earth to sky if this were still the custom in modern society.

All Round the World

Linking the sky with the landscape was a universal activity

Linking with the sky seems to have been part of the human psyche in widely different cultures all round the planet. A solid building on earth then connected to the other half of the landscape - the transparent and moving sky above. We no longer know whether spiritual or symbolic beliefs underlay this fascination with the sky, but the sites themselves act as witnesses that humans have always been interested in time and calendars, the cycles of the sun and moon, surveying and measuring. Noting the key days when the sun and moon could be seen in particular positions on the horizons, it was then natural for them to build their monuments, simple or complex, to link with them visually and therefore to take part in the universal pattern. "As above, so below".

The Great Pyramid, Giza, Egypt (c.2600 BCE).

The sides of its massive structure are aligned North, South, East and West with great precision, which could only be done by astronomical observation. So-called "ventilation-shafts" in the pyramid were also aligned on stars, such as Thuban, the Pole Star at the time, and Orion's Belt which was associated with ancient Egyptian cosmology.

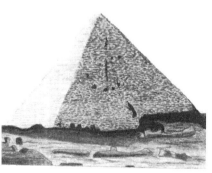

Temple of Concordia, Agrigento, Sicily, Italy (c.500 BCE)

A recent study of ancient Greek temples built in Sicily, such as the magnificent Concordia Temple, showed that 40 out of 41 temples surveyed were aligned to the east, where the sun can be seen to rise twice in the year. The sole exception was a temple dedicated to Hekate, a Moon goddess.

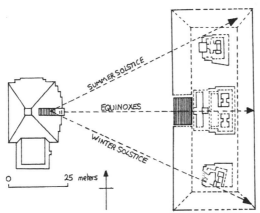

Mayan Astronomical Observatory, Uaxactun, Guatemala (c.500 - 700 CE).

The famous E-group complex of buildings where the three structures on a raised mound mark sunrises at the solstices and equinoxes as seen from a pyramid to the west.

Ancient Circular Structures

All over the world there are ancient circular structures with astronomical alignments built into them. Inevitably they all get labelled as the "Stonehenge" of their particular country!

Goseck Circle
Saxony-Anhalt, Germany (c.4900 BCE).

Goseck is an early example of the many ring ditches discovered in Germany. There are three entrances to the Goseck ring, two aligned to the sunrise (SE) and sunset (SW) at the winter solstice and one in a northerly position.

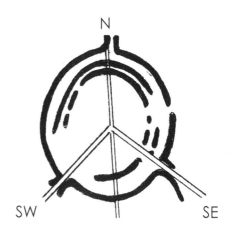

Reconstruction of wooden palisade of Goseck Circle

Rujm el-Hiri,
Golan Heights, Israel (c.3000 BCE).

This so-called "Stonehenge of the Levant" consists of concentric circles formed by thousands of basalt stones, with a mound in the centre. The entrance in the north east marked the summer solstice sunrise.

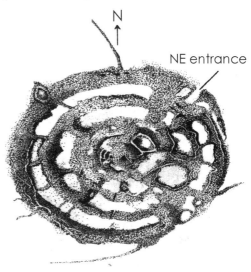

N

NE entrance

Majorville Sun Cairn Ring
Alberta, Canada (c.3000 BCE).

This is "Canada's Stonehenge" a cairn observatory on the prairie, marking the key dates of the solar calendar and the longer lunar cycles.

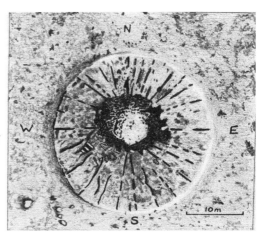

Archaeology

The subject for people who prefer to look down rather than up!

Archaeoastronomers work with sites already listed or "scheduled" by archaeologists, so there can be no argument about their authenticity. Finding the date of prehistoric sites is still an imperfect art, but recent advances in carbon-dating have been helpful. Once the date of a site is known, computers can be employed to recreate images of the sky for the time concerned.

Archaeologists have helped archaeoastronomers by listing, classifying and describing ancient monuments on the web and in County Histories, providing plenty of material to work on. It can also be useful to consult archaeologists if you think that a prehistoric site may have been built over with later structures. For example, a Bronze Age cairn on top of a hill may have been incorporated into an Iron Age hillfort or a large prehistoric burial mound used as the base of a church or castle. During the excavation of a site, archaeologists also often find holes where stones or posts once stood but have been removed, so that a more complete picture of the original structure can be gained.

At present it is unusual for archaeologists to write about the alignment of a stone or other structure, as this is not part of their training. Even when the light of the sun or moon penetrates into a passage mound on a significant date, some have been unwilling until recent years to admit that this was an intentional part of the design. But ideally results from the archaeology and the astronomy should complement each other.

Understanding a Prehistoric Site better by looking at the Astronomy

This cairn at Blaen Glasffrwd in mid-Wales is an example of a site where the astronomy was unrecognised until recently. It looks at first like a random heap of stones but is part of a complex of other cairns and stones carefully set out to incorporate north/south lines and both solar and lunar extremes.

The stone-lined rectangular cist within the cairn points NW towards the summer solstice sunset at the tip of the Lleyn Peninsula over 40 miles away. The cist measures 1 megalithic yard wide, 1 megalithic yard deep and 2 megalithic yards in length (see next page).

Megalithic Measurements

Modern archaeologists generally survey sites using modern metric measurements. However, there has been much research in recent years into ancient measurement systems (metrology). In particular, Professor Thom (see page 72), using his skills as a statistician, showed from his surveys of hundreds of sites that prehistoric people were using their own system of measurements in many parts of Europe, based on a "megalithic yard". The details are given below and it is interesting to test the system out around the perimeters of circles and cairns or any other measurable lengths at sites you visit.

The Megalithic Yard

1 megalithic yard (MY) = 2.722 feet
32.64 inches
82.96 cms.
40 megalithic inches

2.5 megalithic yards = 1 megalithic rod
81.6 inches
100 megalithic inches

2 megalithic yards = 1 megalithic fathom
1 megalithic inch = 2.075 cms.
0.82 inches

Dol de Breton (illustrated opposite).
Largest standing stone in France. Over 30 feet tall.

Megaliths such as this one in Brittany, France, may be striking in the landscape but difficult for archaeologists to deal with using their particular skills. Set in an alignment to mark sunrise on May 8th, which later became the spring festival of St. Michael, it offers insights into the importance of astronomy linked to this special day at the time it was set up. There are also May 8th alignments at Carnac.

Carbon Dating

Until the 1950s much of an archaeologist's time was spent trying to work out the age of sites and artefacts. Time lines were worked out for individual cultures and their histories and then compared with others. There was much disagreement and uncertainty.

However, in 1949 a physicist called Willard Libby found a scientific way of determining the age of carbon-containing remains and this revolutionised the problem of dating archaeological artefacts. His method was based on measuring the rate of decay of carbon 14 in living matter.

For example, a fragment of charcoal or bone found at a site could be analysed in a laboratory and a date given for the death of the plant or animal it derived from. At first there were some mistakes, as with many new scientific breakthroughs, but now carbon dating can be relied on as an accurate, though still expensive, method. The development of

Dol de Breton.

computer technology allowing speedy statistical analysis of huge databases of artefacts has also added to the security of archaeological dating. However, the problem of dating stone (except geologically) still remains.

15

La Hougue Bie, Jersey, Channel Islands (c.4000 BCE)

This fascinating site on Jersey shows how complex the archaeology can be. A huge prehistoric mound, close to sea level has an 18.6 metre long passage in it aligned east/west to the equinox sunrises across the sea over Normandy. Medieval chapels, also aligned east/west were later built on the top of the mound, perhaps unaware of the passage beneath, which had been filled in by then. There were modifications to these chapels in the sixteenth century when they were redesigned as a neo-Gothic "castle" known as the Prince's Tower. Finally this building was in turn demolished and the Germans used the site during World War 2 as an observation point with an underground bunker built into the mound.

Before excavations in the 1990s a concrete access tunnel blocked the entrance to the prehistoric passage, but now it has been sensitively restored so that light once again shines down the passage twice a year as originally designed 6000 years ago.

Plan of the East/West passage and chamber

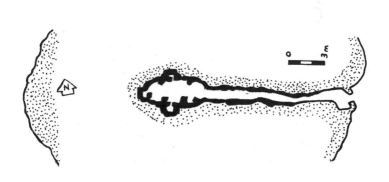

What is Prehistory?

By definition prehistory is any time in history before written records began and this varied from culture to culture. In practice, however, the megalithic monuments that are the main object of study for archaeoastronomers, are chiefly associated with the period of the Neolithic and Bronze Age, from about 4500 BCE.

A Danish museum curator, C.J.Thomsen, first suggested in 1836 a basic terminology for the rough grouping of prehistory into epochs. Originally there were three groups, based simply on whether artefacts were made of stone, bronze or iron. The Stone Age was then further divided into three as follows:

Palaeolithic   from 225,000 BCE (hunter gatherers)

Mesolithic   10,000 – 4400 BCE

Neolithic   4400 – 2300 BCE (farming, pottery, megaliths)

Bronze Age   2300 – 800 BCE   (climate deteriorated by end of epoch)

Iron Age   800 BCE - CE

Stone megalithic monuments cannot themselves be dated except in terms of geology, and so they have been dated according to artefacts found in and around them – which, of course, could sometimes have accrued later. These artefacts are dated by appearance and provenance and also if possible by using carbon dating (see page 14).

 Despite the ruinous nature of many prehistoric sites, however, it is remarkable how their location, design and measurement can still tell us so much about the knowledge and culture of the people who built them. It would be a mistake to think that people who left no written records had not attained an advanced level of culture in other respects.

Masterpieces of Prehistoric Art and Technology

The Nebra Disc

The beautiful Nebra Disc, 32 cms (12.5 ins.) wide, discovered in Germany in 2002 and dating from 1600 BCE is evidence of prehistoric interest in the sky. It depicts stars, including the cluster of the seven Pleiades, as well as sun and moon. The gold strip on the edge of the bronze disc indicates the unique range of the sun's rises and sets along the horizon at the latitude (51.3°) it was found.

The Antikythera Mechanism

This device was found in 1900 amongst the cargo of a ship wrecked near Crete around 65 BCE. It was ignored for nearly a century because no one could believe that such a mechanism could date from so long ago. Now , however, it is acknowledged to be a hand-wound clockwork device used to calculate the motions of the sun, moon and planets as seen from the earth, as well as to predict solar and lunar eclipses.

The levels of astronomy and technology before the modern era should never be underestimated.

Why?

Why did people in the past want to link the sky with the landscape?

There is always a danger that modern people will project their own personalities onto the past. For example, if they are interested in politics, they imagine that in prehistory priests and kings were using their astronomical knowledge to gain power in their communities. Predicting an eclipse, for instance, would be a certain way to impress.

If their interests are in mathematics and science, they imagine prehistoric people designing geometric patterns or working out systems of measurement based on the size of the earth. Sailors presume a practical interest in the skies and astrologers presume that the skies were searched for the understanding of our own personalities and the patterns of the future.

If modern people are religious, they might presume that megalithic sites were places where ancient people came to worship the sun or moon. If they have an idealistic view of human nature they imagine peaceful communities living at one with nature and in tune with the universe.

The truth is most probably that people were much the same as they are now. They were concerned about time and history. They wanted to create calendars, make their mark on the landscape and to commemorate their loved ones who had died. Homo Sapiens has had the same brain size for over 100,000 years, so any of the above ideas could be correct.

What is certain is that studying individual sites in detail is likely to be a better way to share the mindset of their builders than mere imaginative projection.

Ales Stenar (Sweden)

Ales Stenar from the northwest.

Aerial view of the monument.

These stones are arranged in the shape of a ship, with one pointed end marking the rise of the sun at the winter solstice (SE) and the other marking the setting of the sun at the summer solstice (NW). The site is on a grassy headland overlooking the sea on one side and is about 67 metres (73 yards) in length. The date is uncertain, with estimates ranging from 3600 BCE to 600 CE . Whether prehistoric or Viking in origin, however, its shape reflects the cultural traditions of Scandinavia while also linking with the sky.

The example of cup and ring marks below is from Baluachraig, near Kilmartin, Scotland.

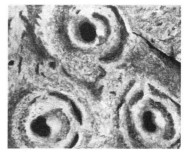

Many questions are still unanswered at megalithic sites, as well as the large philosophical issues. For example, why were cup and ring marks so frequently carved into nearby rocks or on the stones themselves.? Just decorative art? Fresh ideas are needed.

Visual Astronomy

Looking to the horizon, where earth and sky meet

The astronomy of prehistoric people was based on what they could see with their own eyes. So as modern students of the subject, we can do the same and keep the subject simple. Not even a telescope is needed.

Of course, some people, then as now, developed their astronomy more precisely and asked more searching questions about the cycles of the sun and moon, the size of the earth and the way different latitudes could be utilised to capture the movements of the sky more effectively in the construction of their monuments. They worked out ways, for example, to predict eclipses and set up sites that would indicate when the moon was at its extreme positions north and south on the horizon every 18.61 years. The key point, however, about prehistoric astronomy is that it simply depended on observation of the horizons. Records were not in themselves difficult to do and must have been kept over generations of time.

If people today wish to take a scientific, historical or anthropological approach to the subject of archaeoastronomy, then there is endless intellectual interest to be gained. But it is also valuable if people simply go and verify the alignments for themselves, recording and taking photographs. The position of the sun and moon on the horizon has slightly altered over the millennia, but usually not so much that it spoils the drama of the event.

The Thirteen Towers at Chankillo, Peru

A striking example of the use of the horizon for visual astronomy was discovered in recent years in the coastal desert of Peru. Over 2000 years ago (at about 300 BCE) thirteen substantial rectangular structures were built along the horizon, each one with a stone staircase set within it.

The horizon line runs approximately north/south and there are two observation points constructed to the east and west from which the sun could be observed throughout the year rising or setting in the gaps between the structures. The tower at one end marked the summer solstice and at the other end the winter solstice. The toothed horizon, like the back of a huge dormant reptile, could therefore act as an annual solar calendar.

Most aligned prehistoric structures are much simpler, sometimes just marking one significant day in the solar year, but the principle of using the sun on the horizon remains the same.

Rising and Setting Suns and Moons

From a still photograph to animation

Most people consider that the most beautiful sight in nature is a sunrise or sunset. Watching the vivid orange, yellow and red light of the sky beyond the black silhouette of the horizon can be uplifting and awesome.

The moon's rise and set can be just as moving. The full moon always rises at sunset. So, at some sites, after gazing at the sunset in one direction, one can turn round to the opposite horizon and watch the sudden, silent lightening of the sky and the strange white face of the moon appear and rise up into the sky.

Imagine building some of that beauty and dramatic action into a structure which not only gives you an astonishing spectacle but also marks a key point in the annual calendar. Think of these sites as stills from a film which, at the moment in time they were designed for, are suddenly brought to life, by the appearance and movement of the sun or moon as they perfectly combine with the architecture of the stones.

The natural landscape was their artistic medium. There appeared to be no separation between art and science or between spirituality and engineering. This is one of the motivations for getting interested in the subject – not just for the facts to be gained about prehistoric people and their societies but for the sheer beauty of sun and moon on the horizon and the holistic experiences that make one feel part of the massive cycles of the universe.

The Leek Double Sunset

The combination of sun and horizon can sometimes produce strange effects. The first curator of the Ashmolean Museum in Oxford, Dr. Robert Plot, published the top woodcut in 1686 to illustrate the strange phenomenon of the sun setting twice at the summer solstice behind a hill called Bosley Cloud, near Leek in Staffordshire, England.

The observing point is St. Edward's Church, Leek, a medieval church on a hilltop, probably built over a more ancient, pagan site. The series of pictures from the Gentleman's Magazine of 1738 uses rather more artistic licence!

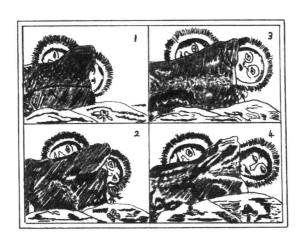

At Ward Hill, Orkney, a double winter solstice sunset can also be seen from Maeshowe passage mound.

North and South

The backbone of a site

Prehistoric people had to establish the north/south line (the meridian) by finding and marking the central (polar) point of the revolving circumpolar stars at night and the highest position of the sun in the daytime.

Today at a new site people often get out their compass to find where the north point is. Alternatively they could try walking a "constant longitude" with a GPS receiver (see page 54) for a few hundred feet, which can give a north/south line accurate to a few minutes of a degree (and similarly walking "constant latitude" can provide an east/west line).

When using a modern compass remember the different definitions of north:

True North is the direction of a line of longitude which converges on the North Pole and which astronomical observation will reveal. This is the north of prehistoric sites.

Grid North is the direction of a grid line on an Ordnance Survey Map. Because of the curvature of the earth, these are never aligned to true north on a flat map. You can see this by matching the same longitude markings on the bottom and top of a map which are angled slightly "off" from the grid lines.

Magnetic North is indicated by a compass and moves slowly over time. Currently it is several degrees west of Grid and True North in Britain. Some Ordnance Survey maps show this variation at the date of the map and there are many websites that can be used to find the current "magnetic declination" at any location. Volcanic rocks also affect the compass.

North/South Alignments

A prehistoric North/South alignment in India.
This stone, framed by two others and aligned to the mountain top due south is in Rola, near Hazaribagh, Jarkhand.

The top of the **Crown Stone.** An extraordinary megalith (25 feet high) in a north/south row of ten at the entrance to the village of Mawsmai, near Cherrapunjee in Meghalaya, one of the north east states of India. Probably erected in the modern era (since 10 CE).

For more information see
www.megalithicsites.co.uk

The North Star

At present the star Polaris is almost exactly north, but the North Star varies over millennia because of precession (the earth`s wobble). To find Polaris, look for the constellation of the Plough (also known as the Great Bear, Big Dipper etc.)

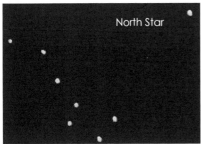

North Star

and follow the line formed by the two pointers. Remember that the Plough revolves counter clockwise around Polaris continuously and so, at different times and seasons, will be seen at other angles in the sky to the one in the diagram.

Horizon and Compass Readings

Why azimuths (compass bearings) are only a starting point

Even when variations in magnetic north and possible local site anomalies are taken into account, a compass is limited in its use in archaeoastronomy. Fortunately for the beauty of the earth's landscape, most of our skylines are formed by the rise and fall of hills, sometimes ascending steeply around a site.

We therefore do not usually see the sun at its furthest point of rise at sea level, but only when it has climbed high enough to be seen over the hills on the horizon. So the azimuth of sunrise or set at the latitude of a site only provides a rough idea of the day an alignment was built to indicate.

Another method besides the use of compass readings is needed to check for a possible astronomical alignment. This involves finding the "declination" of the sun or moon in the sky when it is seen from the site behind a natural or manmade horizon marker (see page 29).

Alignments from sites also only "work" at the latitude of their location (see opposite page). So if comparative analyses between sites are to be undertaken for historical research, then the azimuths must be converted to declinations. Every alignment to the midsummer sunset, for example, will then have a similar declination from which accuracies can be compared.

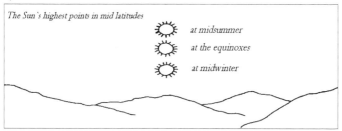

The Sun's highest points in mid latitudes

at midsummer

at the equinoxes

at midwinter

The sun is always due south at its highest point in the middle of the day, but this height varies between summer and winter. The Pole Star in the north at night and the sun at its highest point in the day can therefore both indicate north/south directions.

The Sun on the Horizon (in Northern Latitudes)

In northern mid-latitudes the sun rises around the north east at the summer solstice (about June 21st)and then progressively each day further south until six months later it rises around the south east at the winter solstice (about December 21st). It then moves northwards in its rising position each day until it is back at the summer solstice position six months later.

In between, it rises due east at the equinoxes, around March 21st and September 23rd. Each day it sets along the horizon to the west, so that on the longest day at the summer solstice it rises in the north east and sets in the north west, reaching its annual highest position in the south in the middle of the day. On the shortest day at the winter solstice it rises in the south east and sets in the south west, a much smaller distance to travel, and it is at its annual lowest position in the middle of the day.

One of the obvious ways of establishing that ancient monuments were deliberately aligned to significant horizon points, therefore, is to check that alignments match the particular sun positions at that specific latitude. This shows that the alignment was based on genuine local observation.

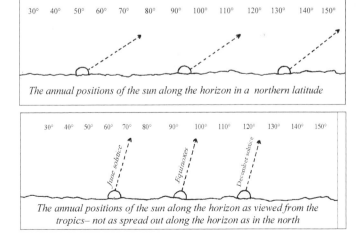

The annual positions of the sun along the horizon in a northern latitude

The annual positions of the sun along the horizon as viewed from the tropics– not as spread out along the horizon as in the north

28

Describing the Sun's Position in the Sky

The meaning of "declination"

Declinations are like latitude lines in the sky along which the sun seems to move from east to west in the course of a day. During the passage of the year, as the earth orbits the sun, the sun seems to rise and fall above and below the celestial equator (0°), a projection into space of the earth's equator. For the summer half of the year its declination increases until midsummer, when it equals the axial tilt angle of the earth (+23°). In winter the declination decreases to the same angle (-23°).

If an alignment therefore points to a particular place on the horizon, a formula can be used, or a declination calculator on a computer, to find the declination of this point where sky meets earth. All you need for this are the co-ordinates (latitude/longitude) and height above sea level (elevation) of both the backsight and foresight. Once the declination is known, it is then clear immediately which day in the solar or lunar cycles the alignment is indicating. The list below shows the chief declinations to look out for.

Being able to find the declination of horizon points is also valuable because it means that the astronomical potential of a site can be worked out theoretically, even if it is impossible to visit it at the right time or if the weather impairs visibility on the horizon at the key moment.

In practice there are certain key declinations to look out for. Unlike azimuths, they do not vary according to latitude. They change only very slowly with the tilt of the earth.

-29°	*Major Lunar Standstill South*
-23°	*Winter Solstice*
-19°	*Minor Lunar Standstill South*
-16°	*Nov. and Feb. Quarter Days*
0°	*Equinoxes*
+16°	*May and Aug. Quarter Days*
+19°	*Minor Lunar Standstill North*
+23°	*Summer Solstice*
+29°	*Major Lunar Standstill North*

Suns Rise and Moon Set

This is a winter solstice sunrise at a site near Pontrhydfendigaid in mid-Wales, seen from a ruined cairn (Declination -23°).

This is an alignment of stones at Aughlish, Co. Derry, Ireland, pointing towards a notch in the horizon where the moon sets at its most southerly extreme at the Major Lunar Standstill (Declination -29°).

Shadow Effects

Visual drama in black and white

Shadows at megalithic sites are the antithesis of beams of sunlight entering passages of mounds, lighting up the rock deep within the earth. Where there is sun and a megalith, there will always be shadows which emphasise more clearly the angle of the sun. On down-sloping ground the shadows elongate further and under snow the visual effect of black on white can be astonishingly dramatic.

To create an aligned site people would set up posts, in line with the correct point on the horizon, and check their positions whenever the day of the alignment reoccurred. Only then would they embark on the huge labour of moving stones. A well-positioned post, often called a gnomon, can show by the movement and size of its shadows the time of the day and year. This is what a sundial also does on a small scale.

As well as shadows of specific stones, a whole site can also be illuminated or thrown into darkness at a sunrise or set. In a bowl of hills, for instance, the light can move down the inner sides of the bowl as the sun rises until certain key stones in the bottom of the valley are the last to be lifted out of shadow. Only by visiting the site regularly can these visual effects be observed and recorded.

**Replica of the George Washington
Sundial Lexington, Kentucky.**

31

Winter Solstice Sunset at Maeshowe on the Orkney Islands, Scotland

At the midwinter sunset– the darkest time of the year-the last rays of the setting sun enter the doorway of Maeshowe passage mound and move into the centre

On the way they cast a shadow pointing to the entrance to the mound from the 10ft high Barnhouse Stone (see right and below).

Summer Solstice Sunset at Castlerigg Stone Circle in the English Lake District.

From the setting sun on the horizon

Shadow Path

The setting sun at the summer solstice casts a shadow path extending hundreds of yards from the tallest stone in the circle. (see picture right) There are also many other sun and moon alignments between stones in the circle and the horizon around.

Equinoxes

Useful calendar points between the solstices

At the solstices the sun appears to move slowly, rising and setting at almost the same positions north or south on the horizon for about four days. Then, half way between the solstices, around March 21st and September 23rd, the sun reaches the point in the sky where it is directly above the equator. It rises in the east and sets in the west as seen from any position on earth.

Prehistoric people clearly noted this and it was useful for them to mark these points, quartering the solar year. Unlike at the solstices, however, the sun seems to move quickly along the horizon at the equinoxes and therefore observations have to be more careful if the precise day is not to be missed.

As well as simply counting the days since the previous solstice, it is probable that they set up posts in an elevated position with horizons of equal altitude to mark the sunrise in the east and then checked that the sun set at the opposite point in the evening. They could do this for several days around the equinox to pinpoint the exact day before "setting it in stone".

In view of the sophistication of the metrology, geometry and astronomical observation at ancient sites, it seems that the challenge of identifying the equinoxes would have caused them no problems. There are certainly many lines of stones set up in an east/west direction, as well as entrances to passage mounds. The beauty of the equinox arrangement is that it works twice in the year.

Equinox Sites

The Temple of the Seven Dolls, Dzibilchaltun, Yucatan, Mexico. Maya temple probably dating from c.700 CE. Viewed from the main causeway the rising sun at the equinox shines brightly through the central door. Many people still gather to see this striking sight.

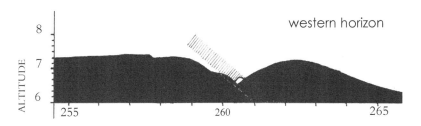

western horizon

ALTITUDE

8
7
6

255   260   265

Brainport Bay, Loch Fyne, Argyll, Scotland. After discovering a summer solstice alignment at this Bronze Age site, archaeologist Dr.Euan MacKie also found that from the same observatory stones a notch in the hills to the west marked the equinox sunset.

Another Equinox Site - The Treasury of Atreus

Every year thousands of tourists visit one of the wonders of the ancient world, known as either the Treasury of Atreus or the Tomb of Agamemnon at Mycenae in Greece. They admire the largest dome in the ancient world, at the time it was constructed in about 1250 BCE. They are also told about the rare coloured stone built into the structure and the possible lining of the walls with precious metals. Archaeologists have never been able to explain, however, why the tomb was placed exactly where it is in relation to the plan of the city and the location of the palace. This can be understood, however, when the triangular window over the entrance is seen as a "light-box" similar to the opening over the entrance at New Grange passage mound in Ireland, which is engineered to let light enter at the winter solstice dawn. In Mycenae the sun rises at the equinoxes over nearby Mount Zara, shines through the triangular window and lights up the far interior wall twice a year, giving a reason for the choice of its exact location in the ancient city.

Nabta Playa, Southern Egypt

First details of this fascinating site in Egypt were published in 1998 and illustrate some of the problems faced by archaeologists and archaeoastronomers. About 24 megaliths in both lines and a small circle in the desert were discovered and carbon dating indicated that the site was used from as far back as 6500 BCE.

There were north/south and east/west alignments and a sightline in a small oval ring that pointed to the summer solstice sunrise. Since the site is close to the Tropic of Cancer, depending on the earth's tilt at the time it was built, it is possible that the builders deliberately looked for the absence, rather than the presence, of shadows at the summer solstice, when the sun would have been directly overhead. Star alignments have also been discovered.

However, possibly to enable a canal project to be completed, the original stones have been moved to a museum and replaced by replicas. The Egyptian government claims that this is to protect them. Therefore a unique megalithic site of great antiquity will be difficult to research in the future since its location, as always, is of crucial importance to its interpretation.

 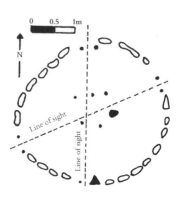

The Tilt of the Earth

(also called the Obliquity of the Ecliptic)

A globe of the earth in its stand is always tilted. The North Pole is not directly on the top and the equator is not horizontal. This is to show the present angle of the earth's axis as it revolves each day. During half the year the northern hemisphere leans away from the sun and then for the other half-year the southern hemisphere is furthest away. This is what causes the seasons, with their longer and shorter days.

At the start of the 21st century, the tilt was at 23° 26' 18", under a minute of a degree less than a century before. Over a very long period of time (about 41,000 years), the tilt changes from about 25° to 21° 30'. It then moves back again.

This alteration in the tilt of the earth affects the position of the sun on the horizon at the solstices. One minute of a degree during a century would hardly be noticed, but over 6000 years, at this rate of one minute per century, there would be a decrease of a whole degree (60 minutes). This is visually twice the sun's own width on the horizon and must therefore be taken into account when watching solstice rises and sets. Indeed it might significantly alter the visual effect of the alignment as originally planned. At sites dated about 4000 BCE the sun should be imagined twice its own width further north while physically watching the solstice rises and sets. Equinox positions are uniquely unaffected and remain accurate over the ages.

The Moving Tropic

Because of the slow changes in the earth's tilt the place where the sun is overhead at the solstice changes over the centuries. This has caused a local problem in a park in Taiwan where a monument was built in 1908 marking the "Northern Line of Return" (i.e. the summer solstice return of the sun) but is now 1.27 km. out of position. Further markers have been added since, but now the park has run out of space to go on commemorating the shifting Tropic of Cancer.

Another device used by people who lived on the Tropic itself was to dig a pit or raise a tower into which the overhead sun would shine to the base only at the solstice. In Central America these were often called "zenith tubes".

Angle of the Ecliptic

This is the angle of the tilt of the earth and changes slowly over time, thus altering the declination of the sun at the solstices. The present angle (still decreasing) is 23.45° but these are some examples from prehistory:

4000 BCE	24.11°
3500 BCE	24.07°
3000 BCE	24.03°
2500 BCE	23.98°
2000 BCE	23.93°
1500 BCE	23.87°
1000 BCE	23.81°

The Fascination of the Moon

Controller of the tides, night-time clock and lantern in the dark

The changeable shape of the moon has fascinated people throughout history. The New Moon can be seen as a thin, slender crescent, near to where the sun has just set, and soon it follows the sun below the horizon. Then each night it rises about 50 minutes later than on the preceding day and moves further away from the sun (by 13.176° on average) across the sky.

After seven nights the New Moon has grown to a half-circle, the First Quarter Moon, and after fourteen nights the moon is full and rises opposite the setting point of the sun. Then it begins to shrink again as it wanes, with the straight edge of its shape now on the other side. It shrinks to a crescent and then disappears for a few days, swallowed up by the glare of the sun.

From Full Moon to the next Full Moon takes on average 29.53 days. It moves 13 times faster than the sun appears to move. The maximum number of nights that the moon can be seen in a month is 28, and its shape is different on every one of them, so it is like a minute hand on a celestial clock, indicating the time of the month while the sun indicates the time of the year.

Parallax

Because astronomical tables always give the position of the moon as if it was being observed from the centre of the earth, a correction has to be applied for the point on the surface of the earth from which a person is watching. Lunar parallax averages at 0.95° and makes the moon rise slightly later and set slightly earlier than predicted.

Monthly changes in the shape of the Moon

From the New Moon on the left, waxing to Full and then
reducing again.

Recumbent Stone Circles and the Summer Full Moon.

Some megalithic monuments were deliberately constructed
to focus on the light of the Full Moon in midsummer in a more
general way than a precise alignment to its rise or set.
Examples can be found in a group of stone circles in north
east Scotland, studied by archaeologist Aubrey Burl, most of
which contain a large recumbent stone, sometimes with tall
flanking stones framing it on either side, towards the south
west of the circle. The Full Moon would be seen moving
above the flat stone horizon of the recumbent stone during
the short midsummer night.

This example of a recumbent stone circle is Easter Aquorthies,
Aberdeenshire, Scotland. The recumbent stone and its two
flanking stones can be seen on the left.

40

Lunar Standstills

Marking the long cycles of the Moon

The idea of a lunar standstill often puzzles people unused to archaeoastronomy, yet is not difficult. Just as the sun reaches its extreme points on the horizon at the solstices, so the moon also has its own extremes when it reaches its widest and narrowest points on the horizon.

The sun takes a year to move steadily each day from its rising and setting positions at its furthest point north in the summer to its furthest point south in the winter and back again. The moon, however, takes 18.61 years from rising and setting each month between its furthest points north and south, gradually reducing its range on the horizon and then returning to the same extreme positions again.

After just over 9 years it rises and sets in the course of a month at its narrowest range on the horizon. When its range of rises and sets is widest, the term "Major Standstill" is used (the last one was in 2006). When its range of rises and sets is at its most narrow, then that period is called the "Minor Standstill".

There are therefore 4 points on the horizon towards the east, marking the lunar standstill rises and 4 points to the west marking the lunar standstill sets (see diagram opposite). Once the full range of the moon's movements were understood, eclipses could be more easily predicted and the changeable patterns of the moon more clearly understood.

Changes in the position of the Moon over 18.61 years.

The diagram on the opposite page of the western horizon shows the extreme setting points of the moon. (In more northern latitudes the range of both lunar and solar settings grows wider. Towards the Tropics the range is narrower.)

Examples of Two Lunar Standstill Sites

Moonset at Callanish

Whoever designed the location and layout of the Callanish stones on the Isle of Lewis, Scotland, was certainly as interested in drama and visual beauty as in astronomy. This picture shows the southern extreme of the full moon at the Major Lunar Standstill, seen from the north of the stones. Before it sets at an azimuth of 203° behind the central megaliths, the moon has risen from and skimmed along a range of hills known as the "Sleeping Beauty" forming the outline of a recumbent woman.

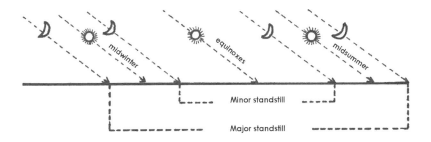

The Octagon Earthworks, Newark, Ohio, USA (200 BCE-500 CE)

The circle and Octagon are part of a much larger group of mounds, banks and roads constructed by the so called "Hopewell" culture. Standing in the circular enclosure and looking along the passage into the octagon, the moon can be seen rising on the horizon beyond at its maximum northern position (Major Standstill) reached every 18.61 years. The curious shape of the octagon and circle allows all the important lunar extremes to be marked as well (see diagram below).

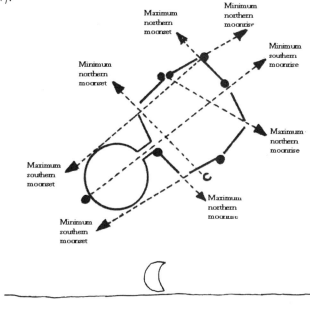

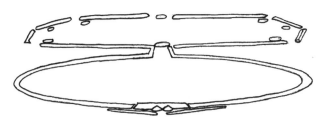

A Hopi Horizon Calendar

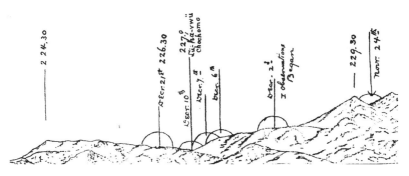

In the 1890s an anthropologist, Alexander M. Stephen made this sketch of the San Francisco mountain range near Flagstaff, Arizona. On it he marked the various sunset positions looked out for by Hopi elders to prepare for their "Soyal" ceremonies close to the winter solstice. When the sun set in the notch on December 10th the Sun Priest could announce that the ceremonies would take place in ten days' time.

Without this contemporary knowledge, however, any alignment to the December 10th notch might be incomprehensible to a modern archaeoastronomer who would be looking for an alignment to the actual solstice. Therefore, it serves as a lesson for how the horizon astronomy needs to be recorded accurately even if the significance is not at first obvious.

Refraction

Refraction is the bending of light rays by the atmosphere. Just as a pencil appears to bend when put in a glass of water, the rays of light from the sun are bent, or refracted, when passing through the earth's atmosphere. In practical terms it is what makes the sun seem to rise earlier and set later than the time given in an almanac. It can also make the sun seem to change shape on the horizon. The beginner does not need to know the physics only to be prepared for the visual distortion and slight time differences caused by refraction at sunrise and sunset.

Reconciling the Sun and the Moon

Solutions to a seemingly insoluble problem

The Sun and the Moon are often thought of as totally different entities like day/night, male/female or yang/yin. The sun's annual cycle of 365.25 days simply does not accommodate a whole number of the moon's months of 29.5 days. 12 lunar months are too few to fit into a solar year and yet 13 months are too many. There are actually 12.368 months in a solar year. It seems that prehistoric people also pondered this problem and wanted to find ways of solving this seemingly intractable difficulty when designing a megalithic site. One approach was to build alignments to both the solar and lunar extremes from the same site so that one place served to mark them both equally. But an even more satisfying solution was through geometry, using a right-angled triangle.

Archaeoastronomer Robin Heath has shown that a rope with 30 equal spaces marked on it, for example with knots, can be pegged out to make a right-angled triangle with sides of 5, 12 and 13 of the unit of measure chosen. Lowering the 13 side of the triangle to the 3:2 ratio point of the 5 side will then make the internal measurement of the rope 12.368, which is the number of lunar months in a solar year. The extra piece of rope protruding beyond the 5 side then represents the 10.875 days which have to be added to 12 lunar months to equal a solar year.

This length of 10.875 days also has the same ratio to the lunation period of 29.5 days as an English foot (12 inches) has to the megalithic yard (2.72 feet). See page 13 for table of prehistoric measures. So both astronomical and metrological knowledge were encoded together in the triangle.

Lunation Triangles Large and Small

The Station Stone rectangle at Stonehenge consists of two 5/12/13 triangles and across the southern countryside of Britain Robin Heath discovered a huge 5/12/13 triangle, 2500 times larger, linking Stonehenge, Lundy Island and the unique Bluestone quarry site in the Preseli hills.

The 3:2 ratio point on the 5 side of this landscape triangle falls on Caldey Island. Bringing bluestones to Stonehenge would have drawn attention to this great triangle and therefore also to this brilliant way of encapsulating the relationship of the solar and lunar cycles in a geometric form. There is certainly no more convincing theory to explain why the Welsh blue-stones were brought to Stonehenge.

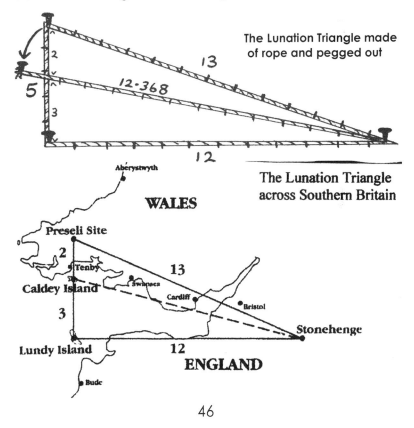

The Lunation Triangle made of rope and pegged out

The Lunation Triangle across Southern Britain

Seeing Stars

The sites need to be dated precisely first

If the people who built the prehistoric sites were watching carefully the movements of the sun and moon, then naturally it can be assumed that they were observing the stars as well. Very few stars are bright enough to see on the actual horizon, but they would have been observed at least for night-time navigation and to mark the seasons.

However, for modern archaeoastronomers, connecting sites to stars is difficult because as yet archaeologists are imprecise about the dating of many prehistoric monuments. In the last twenty years, the accepted dates of some sites have been put back by thousands of years. So, although computer programmes can instantly show what the sky looked like at any point in history from any location, this information is limited without a sure dating. The sun and moon have moved only about a degree along the horizon in the last 6000 years, so those alignments are still visually close today but, due to precession, it is possible for stars to move a degree in about a hundred years.

Sometimes other factors support the case for star alignments, however. One example is when a site is laid out in the pattern of a familiar constellation or asterism such as Orion's Belt, which seems to be mirrored on the ground in several places around the world including at the Thornborough Henges in Yorkshire, illustrated opposite.

Orion's Belt on the ground: Thornborough Henges

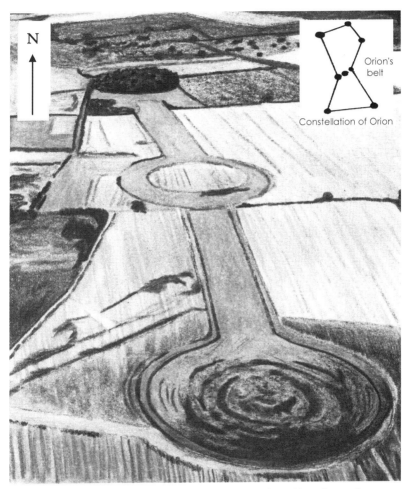

The Thornborough Henges (c3000 BCE) mirror the stars of Orion's Belt in their layout, with one star offset from the line. The three pyramids at Giza in Egypt are arranged in a similar pattern as well as other prehistoric sites across the world. The constellation of Orion is a striking feature of the winter skies over Britain.

Extinction Angles of Stars and Precession

Be prepared for the fact that stars are invisible within a few degrees of the horizon as they rise or set. Even the brightest stars such as Sirius can only be seen on the horizon in exceptional conditions. This is why it is unlikely that stone alignments linked up with a star's appearance on the actual horizon, although obviously we can assume that the stars were familiar to people in prehistory and would have been used for navigation on sea and land. Watch the horizons at sunset or sunrise and test this out for yourself under different weather conditions.

An artificial raised horizon in the form of a bank or part of a long barrow may have been used instead to overcome the visual limitation of the more distant horizon. This is certainly one explanation for the strange shape of some early barrows such as Fussell's Lodge or Wayland's Smithy in southern England. The passages inside are usually short and placed at one end. The rest of the long, sloping, wedge-shaped mounds, often with banks and ditches along the sides, seems therefore to be practically unnecessary. However, if they were used to block the distant horizons and form a closer artificial barrier to look over at star rises, this could explain their strange design.

Precession

Over 25,920 years there is a slight wobble in the axis of the earth as it rotates. In practical terms the effect of this is for the position of some stars against the background of the zodiac (on the ecliptic) to move slowly around the horizon as it rises or sets by about one degree in a hundred years.

What kind of person would make a good archaeoastronomer?

Important qualifications:

- Curiosity about megalithic sites and a real desire to understand why they were built and why they were placed exactly where they are.

- Enjoyment in getting out on the hills and moors where so many of the remaining sites can be found. If your fitness levels are not great, however, then you can always concentrate on sites close to roads.

- Willingness to read up books on archaeology, ancient history and gazetteers of sites. But you don't need a degree or other academic qualification – indeed these are often handicaps. An open mind is more useful.

- Willingness to learn and grasp some very basic visual astronomy, as described in this book. If you get interested, you can always study more and therefore discover more, but general knowledge is enough to get started.

- It helps if you are happy to use some simple equipment such as a map, a camera, a compass, a calculator, a computer (to save yourself some basic maths and to keep up to date on new discoveries) and preferably a handheld GPS receiver used by walkers. If a theodolite is a step too far, then leave one of those to the specialists.

.

Adopt a Site
Become the authority on one chosen place

If you think that some feature at a site is aligned with a significant point on the horizon such as a natural notch or built cairn, you need to know what the declination of the sun or moon would be when seen at that point. Start by using the diagram of azimuths illustrated opposite to guess which astronomical event the suspected alignment may point to. Then ideally visit the site on the appropriate day (e.g. a solstice) to see it rise or set with your own eyes. Remember, though, that the sun will now be about half a degree further south from its position in, for example, 2500 BCE.

But because our lives are busy and the weather is unreliable, a theoretical method is also needed. For this you will have to go to each end of the alignment and read off from your GPS (or map if necessary) the exact co-ordinates of latitude and longitude and the site's elevation above sea level. If the horizon feature is a long way off, you may have to get the GPS reading for that point on another day.

Then later at home you can feed the GPS figures into a

computer programme, such as those suggested on www.skyandlandscape.com. The computer will then tell you the solar and lunar declinations at the horizon point and therefore which day is marked by the alignment. In practice you can get into the habit of collecting GPS readings while out walking and keeping them in a notebook for future use.

The Long Man of Wilmington, Sussex. Prototype archaeo - astronomer with surveying poles?

51

Possible Alignments to Look For at a Site

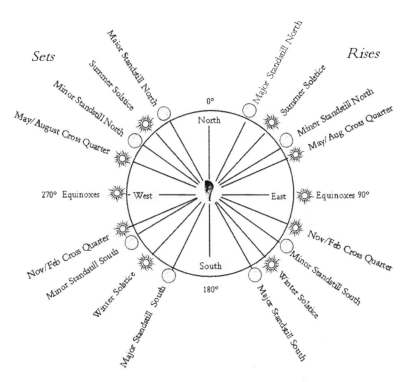

As a starting point it is useful to make a diagram similar to the one above for individual sites, writing in the azimuths (compass bearings) for the various possible solar and lunar horizon positions at a chosen latitude. It is likely that only a few of the points will be visible at any individual site and, of course, the azimuths will alter according to the rise and fall of the horizons. But it is a reminder of some of the possible alignments to look out for.

Dividing the Year

Dates to put in your diary for visiting your chosen sites

Even if you work out theoretically when the sun or moon will "activate" a particular site, there is no substitute for being there in person, especially at sunrise and sunset, as often as possible. You may also discover other unexpected alignments.

The key days to visit; however, are:

midsummer solstice   around June 21st,

midwinter solstice   around December 21st

one of the equinoxes   around March 21st or September 23rd

or one of the so-called Quarter Days – the Celtic festivals of

Imbolc   February 1st

Beltane   May 1st

Lammas   August 1st

Samhain   November 1st

These may fall on different dates each year, so ideally an almanac, newspaper or internet site should be consulted to find the exact days as well as the times of sunrise and sunset. (N.B. when working out the time of day for sunrise or sunset add one hour for each 15° west of Greenwich and subtract one hour for each 15° east).

During the extreme rises and sets of the major and minor standstills of the moon, it is worth watching every moonrise from a site when the moon is near its monthly maximum or minimum declination. In addition rising Full Moons (opposite the sunset) are always worth watching throughout the year just for the visual impact of the sight!

GPS and Theodolite

GPS (Global Positioning System) Receiver

(about the size of a mobile phone)

As well as helping to guide walkers over the hills, one of these handheld devices is very useful for field work in archaeoastronomy. You can read off the latitude and longitude of your position, your height above sea level and even the times of sunrise and set. When you have recorded the co-ordinates and elevation of two points on an alignment, use a computer programme such as GetDec (downloadable from Leicester University Archaeology Dept. website) to find the declination of the horizon point. To do this you will have to convert the grid references or co-ordinates into TM format first (Transverse Mercator)– but there are converters on the web for this. See also the Learning Tools section of **www.skyandlandscape.com** for further help and advice.

A Theodolite

This is not an essential purchase for the beginner, but will prove useful eventually if you want more precise data and especially if you are sighting over long distances. However, for archaeoastronomy it is not necessary to buy the latest, most expensive model. Its main disadvantage is its weight if it has to be carried far over rough terrain. But its readings are more accurate than those of a GPS, from which in turn it is easier to gain precision than from any map. Lighter-weight theodolites have also recently come on to the market if you do decide to invest in one some day.

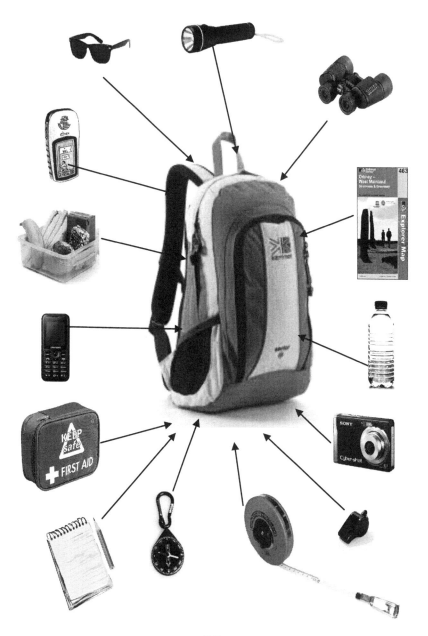

Equipment for Archaeoastronomy work in the field

It's very easy to forget some crucial piece of equipment and to discover its absence when you are miles away from anywhere on a remote piece of moorland. So here is a checklist:

- **Rucksack**
- **Maps** (OS maps to cover whole area. Why is the megalith always on the edge of the map?)
- **GPS** (with spare batteries)
- **Notebook and pencil** for noting down co-ordinates and elevations – unless you prefer to use your mobile phone.
- **Compass**
- **Binoculars**
- **Sun glasses** (remember not to stare directly at the sun)
- **Tape measure** – as long as possible.
- **Torch and whistle** – remember you have to get down from the hills when the sun has disappeared below the horizon and that the moon often rises a long time after the sun has set.
- **Camera** – take lots of pictures from every angle.
- **Mobile phone** – though don't forget that there is often no signal in remote areas.
- **Water and snacks.** Your outings will be so interesting that you will stay out longer than planned.
- **First Aid kit.**
- **Wear good footwear** for rough walking and take waterproofs and warm clothing even in summer.
- **Take a companion** with you if at all possible, even if they grumble a lot. Remind them that at least they are not yet being asked to carry a theodolite. That comes later!

Eclipses
Grand astronomical dramas

An eclipse of the moon and, even more, of the sun can be a startling and disturbing sight. Without warning the moon seems to have lost a slice from one side or is blotted out by a red-brown shadow. At a solar eclipse the sun starts to go dark, birds stop singing and there is a strange sense of nature in suspension. So in a society which observed the sky closely, much thought and effort would naturally be spent to understand and predict these strange events.

Eclipses only occur at those Full or New Moons when the earth, moon and sun are all in the same plane in the sky, or close to the same in the case of partial eclipses. At a solar eclipse the New Moon blocks some or all of the sun and at a lunar eclipse the shadow of the earth darkens some or all of the Full Moon. The difficulty is that an eclipse does not always occur at these times. Usually the moon, earth and sun are not quite on the same plane so do not block the light of each other.

To predict an eclipse, therefore, the cyclic patterns of all three have to be observed closely to prepare for possible "danger" times when some form of eclipse might be likely. Then, when an eclipse occurred, it would confirm the reasoned speculation and make the predictions of future eclipses still more accurate.

The Aubrey Holes and Eclipses

Within the henge bank at Stonehenge are 56 filled-in pits which John Aubrey first noted. Various theories have been put forward to explain the original function of these holes.

One is that they could have been used to record solar and lunar cycles, by moving markers from one pit to the other – the moon marker twice a day (completing the circle in about a lunar month) and the sun marker two holes every 13 days (completing the circle in about a year).

Correcting slightly, perhaps at new moons and at solstices and equinoxes, this is an effective working calendar, visually integrating the sun and moon. When the two markers were together at new moons, or opposite at full moons, this method would also have assisted in the prediction of potential eclipses

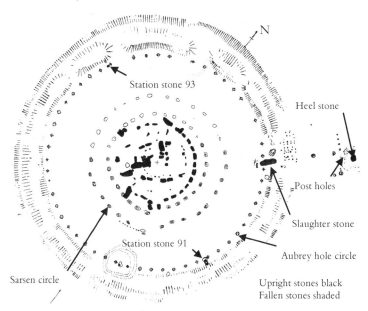

**Professor Thom`s 1973 survey of Stonehenge.
The Aubrey holes are just within the henge bank.**

Precision Astronomy
The greatest coincidence of all would be ...
......that they are all coincidences!

The ruins of ancient sites with their fallen and missing megaliths, deserted and overgrown, make it seem now that the builders operated in a slapdash manner, carelessly setting up stones on unlevelled ground in undistinguished settings. However, clues often remain to indicate whether the builders were working on a far more "scientific" basis than might first appear. The size of the engineering project in building the site is one clue about the sophistication and organising capability of the makers. Massive stones are clearly harder to move than small ones and yet the builders often did not hesitate to transport stones over long distances for reasons we no longer understand.

Using a specific measurement system is also a clue to the thinking of the builders. Perimeters of circles and cairns are often found to be in whole numbers of megalithic yards or rods. There may also be other features such as cists, or distances between stones that are still measurable.

As far as stone circles are concerned, look out for complex geometry. It is comparatively easy to make a perfect circle, but many circles are actually constructed by more complicated methods (see opposite).

For the beginner there is no need to delve into geometry and metrology at once, but you will probably get interested before long. If a site has been constructed on careful geometric principles and using a uniform system of measurement, then it is likely that the builders would also be asking precise questions about astronomy beyond the obvious ones to establish an annual solar calendar.

Geometry of Stone Circles

Actual circles, which are comparatively easy to construct with a rope and peg, comprise about two thirds of the stone circles found in Britain. Others are more complicated and an indication of the mathematical inventiveness of their builders. Here are some examples taken from Megalithic Sites in Britain by Professor Alexander Thom:

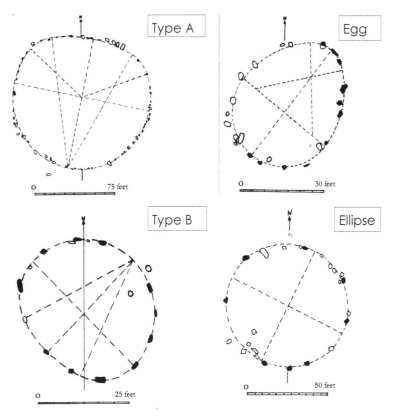

Type A : Dinnever Hill (Stannon), Bodmin Moor, Cornwall.
Type B : Bar Brook, Derbyshire.
Egg : Allan Water (Burgh Hill) , Roxburghshire, Scotland.
Ellipse : Penmaen Mawr (Druids Circle), North Wales.

Seafaring and Astronomy

When knowledge of the skies could save your life

Seafaring is probably as old as the human race, but can certainly be presumed from the Mesolithic period onwards (from c.10,000 BCE) based on the widespread distribution of trade goods such as axes, pottery and raw materials such as tin. Cowries from the Maldives, for example, have been found in prehistoric tombs in Finland. Ancient maps such as the Piri Reis also suggest that navigational surveying was being practised with accuracy before the Antarctic was frozen over (before c.4000 BCE).

Making a calendar and navigating a ship require the same kind of knowledge of the skies. So prehistoric monuments aligned to the sky have been described as "almanacs in architecture". For a sailor, travelling long distances in a small boat before the days of magnetic compasses and sextants, knowledge of the sky would have been a matter of life and death. It is far more dangerous to hug the coastline in a ship than to get out into the open sea, using the sun, moon and stars as guides. However, when they did come ashore, there was also an urgent necessity for early mariners to understand the relationship of the moon to tides.

There are detailed accounts even in recent times of sailors without modern technology using the skies for navigation - in Polynesia, for example. We also know from the pioneering work of Thor Heyerdahl and others that boats can be constructed with simple technology and sailed successfully across the oceans, using the prevailing currents. If the capacity for long-distance sea travel in the prehistoric world can be accepted, however, then why not the use of astronomical alignments on the land?

Astronomy and Navigation in the South Seas

An example of how the Polynesians used the rigging of their boats to line up stars for the voyage to a particular island.

**From a sketch by David Lewis
(We, the Navigators) 1972**

In the Gilbert Islands until recent times "Stone Canoes" were used for instruction, both to learn about the appearance of waves out at sea and also to observe and memorise the stars rising in a particular direction throughout the night. Perhaps some of the seemingly random stones found at megalithic sites around the world were used in the same way?

Seagoing ships built with Stone Age Technology

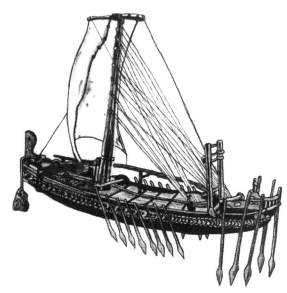

Model of a sea-going ship of Egyptian Pharaoh Sahure (c.2490 BCE)

A replica of Thor Heyerdahl`s famous raft, the Kon Tiki, that sailed from Peru halfway across the Pacific in 1947. His experiment has since been replicated many times.

The Pyramid Boat at Giza

Around the Great Pyramid of Giza archaeologists have discovered huge pits, some empty but one containing 1224 parts of a large ship built before about 2500 BCE. This has now been reconstructed and is on display in a special Boat Museum at the site. The ship was made of Lebanese cedar and some acacia wood. It is 43.3 metres long and 5.9 metres wide.

The boats buried around the pyramid may have been symbolic or only used for the Pharaoh's river travel, not long-distance journeys over the oceans. But the complexity and sophistication of their design indicates the advanced technology of the ancient Egyptian boat-builders.

Model of Pyramid boat

Latitude and Longitude
Astronomy naturally leads to mapping the earth

It is probable that thinking people understood that the earth was round from time immemorial, despite the fact that the Church tried for its own reasons to deny this in the Middle Ages. People would see the curve of the distant horizon, watch the mast of a ship seem to gradually sink below the sea as it sailed away or observe a mountain top rear up as they travelled closer. They would also observe the roundness of the sun and moon and see the arc of the earth's shadow move across the moon at a lunar eclipse.

When out at sea no doubt they could "sail the parallel" (i.e. sail in a straight line along the latitude) just as well as Columbus and later explorers could do. Two thousand years ago Ptolemy on his maps and in his Geography gave the approximate latitude and longitude of thousands of places, using a longitude line through the Canary Islands as his Prime Meridian (the modern one goes through Greenwich).

They could also ascertain Latitude by measuring the height of the Pole Star, or its equivalent point in the centre of the circumpolar stars. The elevation angle of the Pole is the same as latitude at any given place (see below).

Then, once the ideas of latitude and longitude were accepted for the planet as a whole, it would be natural to develop a grid system for mapping and measuring particular land areas. This large scale surveying is certainly evident in Britain from the location of important sites.

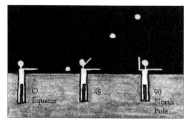

The North Star and Latitude

At the North Pole (90° north latitude) the Pole Star is directly overhead. At the Equator (0° latitude) it sits on the horizon. In just the same way, in mid-latitudes, the number of degrees of the angle of the Pole Star to the horizon is the same as the latitude of the place it is measured from

Prehistoric Travel and Surveying

Currents and prevailing winds could have acted as conveyor belts across the oceans for prehistoric navigators and explorers as illustrated below.

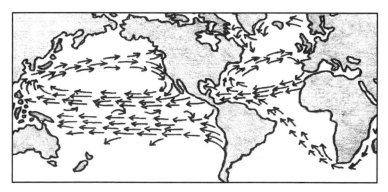

There is also more evidence for the careful placing of prehistoric sites in larger landscape areas, as in the map below. It is clear that not only do archaeologists need to look up at horizons, but also to consider that serious surveying was being practised in prehistory. GPS devices enable anyone now to check the co-ordinates at sites all over the country and investigate prehistoric surveying for themselves.

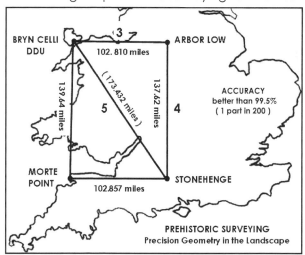

PREHISTORIC SURVEYING
Precision Geometry in the Landscape

Courtesy of
Robin Heath
April 2008

Pioneers of Archaeoastronomy
Aubrey, Stukeley, Lockyer and Thom

Many influential people have made special contributions to this subject.

John Aubrey (1626 – 1697) was a member of the newly-formed Royal Society at the end of the 17th century and had an open enquiring mind which he applied to everything around him. In particular he managed to interest Charles II in Stonehenge and Avebury and this royal approval encouraged others to study British ancient monuments.

Rev. William Stukeley (1687 – 1765) left a large number of engravings of ancient sites which were popular in his day and which have served as a useful record of many sites since altered or destroyed.

Sir Norman Lockyer (1836 – 1920) was the Astronomer Royal with a distinguished academic career in astronomy. Then, in his fifties, he also became interested in the astronomical alignments of ancient buildings – Greek and Egyptian sites as well as British. He recorded his findings meticulously and archaeologists have still to catch up with his extensive work.

Professor Alexander Thom (1894 – 1985), a Professor of Engineering at Oxford University, has made such an exceptional contribution to the subject that it is difficult to summarise his achievements. He combined the highest academic standards in engineering, surveying, mathematics, statistics and astronomy with a single-minded determination to understand megalithic structures. He formulated the "megalithic yard" and "megalithic month", recorded the complex geometry of stone circles and discovered the astronomical alignments of hundreds of sites whilst producing the first professional surveys of most of them. And all of this was done in his spare time!

The Value of Recording and Measuring

This is William Stukeley's eighteenth century engraving of a dolmen called the Shelving Stones north of Avebury. It has since been destroyed so is an example of the importance of exact recording of sites, whichever age one lives in.
John Aubrey in the seventeenth century made a plan of Avebury containing eighty stones; a hundred years later Stukeley recorded seventy and now there are about fifty.

Unfortunately, modern work in archaeoastronomy has largely concentrated on the statistical likelihood of alignments being deliberate rather than coincidental. It has even been suggested that archaeoastronomers should be trained in the application of mathematical probability theories such as Bayes Theorem.

This has diverted attention from the most useful activity of all – obtaining measurements, plans, photographs and written records of megalithic sites to prevent knowledge being lost for the future.

When you have collected sufficient new evidence about a site, send it to your local newspaper, historical society or a website that will accept new material on ancient sites.

Carnac and Current Research

Astronomy, geometry and symbolism
perfectly combined

The Carnac region of Brittany is the largest and most complex megalithic site in the world. Best known for thousands of large standing stones arranged in rows, the area also contains hundreds of dolmens, decorated passage graves as at Gavrinis, vast tumuli, single tall standing stones and stone circles (cromlechs). These use the same geometry and units of length as those found throughout Britain.

The Grand Menhir Brise at Locmariaquer, now lying broken into three pieces, once stood over 65 feet tall and weighed over 340 tons.

One site in particular combines astronomy, geometry and the symbolism of human procreation. At Le Manio a complex arrangement of triangles and quadrilateral is focussed around a 20 foot stone called Le Geant, whose shadow at the equinox falls on a rotund recumbent stone called La Dame du Manio, whose shape resembles that of a pregnant woman. Nine months later, at the winter solstice, the shadow then falls through the vulva-like gap between the two largest stones of the quadrilateral, where it marks the (re) birth of the Sun at midwinter.

The angular difference (36.8°), unique to the latitude of Carnac, is marked on the ground by a 3-4-5 Pythagorean triangle, one of two at the site, and there are also two 5-12-13 triangles, all in units of megalithic yards or rods (2.5MY).

Miraculously the quadrilateral remains in good condition and has recently been accurately surveyed and shown to contain alignments to important solar and lunar rises which aid the start and finish 'counts' for two lunation triangles (see page 46) which 'marry' solar and lunar cycles.

Le Manio, Carnac

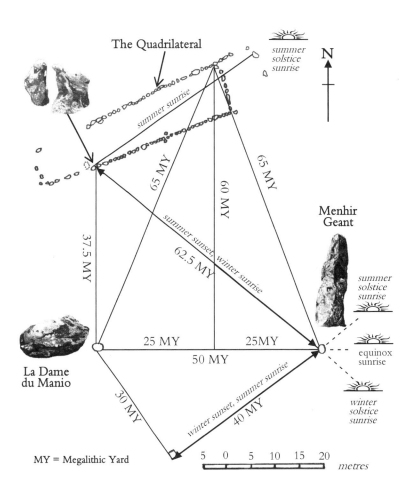

The Quadrilateral

summer
solstice
sunrise

N

summer sunrise

65 MY

65 MY

60 MY

37.5 MY

summer sunset, winter sunrise

62.5 MY

Menhir
Geant

summer
solstice
sunrise

equinox
sunrise

25 MY   25MY

50 MY

La Dame
du Manio

winter sunset, summer sunrise

30 MY   40 MY

winter
solstice
sunrise

MY = Megalithic Yard

5   0   5   10   15   20

metres

Survey plan courtesy of Howard Crowhurst and Robin Heath

70

Continuation of the Tradition

Astronomical alignments still have a role to play

When the great cathedrals and abbeys of Europe were designed in the Middle Ages, often on prehistoric sites, their architects paid close attention to the way the light would fall to illuminate the stained glass and accentuate the lines and details of the buildings. Sometimes, however, they went further, as at Chartres Cathedral, France, where a clear pane of glass in the window of "Saint Apollinaire", depicting the Roman sun god Apollo, allows a ray of light to fall on a marked tile in the floor on the summer solstice each year (see top illustration below).

Modern cities are very congested and so architects today rarely have the luxury of being able to choose a position where their building can be angled to capture light at an appropriate time of the year. Sometimes, however, they have been given this opportunity and have constructed some striking examples of linking the sky with their designs. One example is the plan for the reconstruction of the World Trade Centre site after the attack on September 11th 2001 in New York. It includes the idea of solar alignments to mark the times when the plane hit the first tower at 08:46 am and when the second tower collapsed at 10:28 am. The Wedge of Light is a triangular piazza whose shape is defined by the angles of the sun at these key moments.

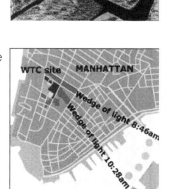

When momentous personal and national events are remembered, the link with the sky creates a sense of universal significance even today.

Linking with the Sky in the Modern World

The Armed Forces Memorial, Lichfield, England

At the National Arboretum near Lichfield in the centre of England the Armed Forces Memorial, dedicated in 2007, follows the pattern of many prehistoric sites. It is situated on a mound with a circular path around it and it consists of outer and inner walls, one within the other, designed to hold the names of Service men and women who have been killed since the Second World War. Most of all on Remembrance Day, at the eleventh hour of the eleventh day of the eleventh month, a ray of light shines through deliberately constructed gaps in the walls and falls onto the central point where there is a wreath of poppies carved in stone.

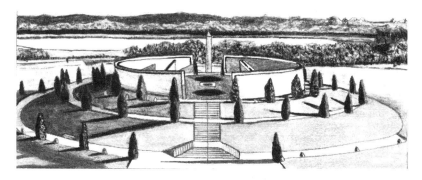

The Armed Forces Memorial is reminiscent of the world- famous passage mound at New Grange in Ireland, where the sun shines through a specially constructed "light box" at sunrise on the winter solstice, illuminating the decorated passage within. (c.3000 BCE)

New Grange , Ireland

Moving the subject forward

It's far too fascinating to be kept as a secret for the few!

The internet has made it possible for anyone to find out about new prehistoric sites and it is clear that there are megalithic circles, rows, dolmens and cairns in whichever country is investigated. This is not surprising, of course, if one accepts that the sky has always been a source of knowledge and myth until modern industrialised societies moved indoors, acquired clocks and drew their curtains on the moon and stars, if not the sun!

Another reason for archaeoastronomy to become more widely studied at the present time is the development of computer programmes to do any mathematics required. People from all backgrounds are drawn to megalithic sites and now they can take the next step forward and start the process of establishing why that place was chosen. What do the horizons indicate? Most of all they can share the excitement of their ancestors in watching for the rise and set of sun or moon on the right day in the right place.

Much modern archaeoastronomy has concentrated on ways to prove beyond doubt the authenticity of astronomical alignments, using probability theories and complex testing. But ultimately the best way to convince doubters is to find so many sites that link with the sky that the cumulative evidence will be overwhelming.

Now is the time for everyone moved by these sites to play their part by helping to collect information: photos, diagrams, reports, measurements or astronomical alignments. Prehistoric archaeology will be changed for good.

The M'Soura Ellipse, Morocco. (c.1800 BCE)

Sites all round the world are waiting for further detailed examination. This remarkable tumulus, surrounded by a ring of megaliths, is in the Lavache Region of Northern Morocco. Its site has been carefully chosen so that alignments can be made to the solar and lunar extremes over the Rif Mountains in the east. The tallest megalith, El Outed, is nearly 20 feet (about 6 metres) high.

El Outed (The Pointer)

El Outed in its setting

Extra Information

Much detective work can be done at home

There are many books on prehistoric sites all round the world, sometimes with such wonderful photographs in them that you want to jump up at once to go and visit them. However, unless you have unlimited time and money you cannot spend your life travelling around visiting them all. So get all the information you can from other sources. There are fascinating books on prehistory and archaeology, local guide books and reference books for particular types of monument (e.g. stone circles). Sometimes old books in second hand bookshops can also tell you about stones that were once standing but have now been removed to make a new road or build a new bungalow.

Get all the maps you can find (old and new) that contain your chosen site or area and study them closely.

Look on the web for measurement converters, sunrise and sunset tables, almanacs and details of prehistoric monuments etc.

Look out also for webcams set up at some famous sites to watch the sun or moon at solstices or standstills, so that you can observe the event from the comfort of your own home.

Remember that you can also get Apps for your mobile phone to identify the night sky and sometimes even use your phone for some of the relevant calculations.

Examples of Azimuths of Solstices and Lunar Standstills

This table shows the range of horizon positions of the sun and moon at a variety of latitudes. The moon`s azimuths are obtained by adding the figure in the "lunar angle" column on the left for Major Standstills and subtracting it for Minor Standstills.

Latitude	Lunar	Summer solstice		Winter solstice	
of site	angle	(SS) R = rise, S = set		(WS) R = rise, S = set	
	+ and −				
(degrees)	(degrees)	(azimuth 0)			(azimuth 0)
		SSSR	SSSS	WSSR	WSSS
30 Giza	5.93	62.05	297.94	11 7.89	242.11
40 Greece	6.71	58.ol	302.00	121.92	238.08
45 Bordeaux	7.27	54.97	305.02	124.95	235.08
48 Carnac	7.68	52.66	307.34	127.25	232.74
50 Cornwall	8.00	50.85	309.15	129.06	230.94
51 Stonehenge	8.17	49.84	310.15	130.06	229.94
52 Rollrights	8.35	48.76	311.23	131.14	228.86
53 Derby	8.54	47.60	312.40	132.30	227.70
54 Lancaster	8.74	46.34	313.66	133.56	226.44
55 Carlisle	8.96	44.97	315.03	134.93	225.07
56 Edinburgh	9.19	43.47	316.53	136.4)	223.58
57 Aberdeen	9.44	41.83	318.17	138.05	221.95
58 Ullapool	9.70	40.02	319.98	139.85	220.15
59 Orkneys	9.98	38.00	321.99	141.85	218.14
60 Lerwick	10.28	35.74	324.25	144.10	215.89

The table assumes that the horizon is flat and is calculated for about 2500 BCE.

(courtesy of Robin Heath)

Bibliography

Below is a short, highly selective list of possible books that you might want to buy or borrow from a library to start with.

There are various points to make, however, before you begin. First, books on prehistoric archaeology may describe sites, discuss chronologies and make guesses about the type of society that produced aligned monuments but don't expect references to astronomy. Most archaeologists simply do not look at the monuments in the context of their landscape settings. Prehistoric archaeology books can therefore tell you many facts about your chosen site and the other monuments in the area, but you will almost always have to add the astronomy yourself.

If you are not a mathematician or astronomer, be prepared too for the fact that specialist books on archaeoastronomy can often look difficult to comprehend, but don't be put off by the sight of equations on a page. Approach the subject a little at a time and then gradually look in these books to find answers to your questions as they arise.

My suggestion is that you begin with reference books to particular types of site or particular countries and areas. For example, Aubrey Burl's books on stone circles or rows of standing stones will always be useful and will give you ideas about places to visit and what to expect when you reach a site. County histories often include lists of ancient sites as well.

There are very few general astronomy books in this list, because the geocentric astronomy needed to appreciate the prehistoric sites involves a different approach to that of modern astronomers. But, of course, the greater your knowledge of the skies, the more you will enjoy getting out of doors and watching sun and moon rises and sets.

There is also an international journal produced in America,

simply called *Archaeoastronomy*, which issues occasional editions, mostly about sites in the Americas.

The list below is subjective and deliberately short since it is designed for beginners. However, some of the scholarly works referred to contain extensive bibliographies which you can browse through later if you want. Be aware, also, that many of these books are now out of print and you will therefore have to search for second hand copies.

General Archaeological Reference books:

Burl, Aubrey (1993). *From Carnac to Callanish. The Prehistoric Stone Rows and Avenues of Britain, Ireland and Brittany*. New Haven and London: Yale University Press.

Burl, Aubrey (1995). *A Guide to the Stone Circles of Britain, Ireland and Brittany*. New Haven and London: Yale University Press.

Canby, Courtlandt (1988). *A Guide to the Archaeological Sites of the British Isles*. New York and Oxford: A Hudson Group Book. (old but useful gazetteer)

 Cope, Julian (1998). *The Modern Antiquarian*. London: Thorsons. (a subjective and unacademic presentation of a wide range of prehistoric sites, with fascinating photographs).

Cope, Julian (2004). *The Megalithic European*. London: Element. (as above – quirky and personal but lavishly illustrated).

Harding, Jan (2003). *Henge Monuments of the British Isles*. Stroud, Gloucestershire: Tempus.

Service, Alastair and Bradbery, Jean (1981). *A Guide to the Megaliths of Europe*. St.Albans: Granada.

General introductory reading:

Aveni, Anthony (2008). *People and the Sky. Our Ancestors and the Cosmos*. London: Thames and Hudson.

Bauval, Robert and Gilbert, Adrian (1994). *The Orion Mystery. Unlocking the Secrets of the Pyramids.* London: Heinemann. (an example of the many books on Egyptian archaeoastronomy).

Brennan, Martin (1994). *The Stones of Time (Calendars, Sundials and Stone Chambers of Ancient Ireland).* Inner Traditions Bear and Company.

Brown, Peter Lancaster (1976). *Megaliths, Myths and Men. An Introduction to Astro-Archaeology.* Mineola, New York: Dover Publications, Inc.

Burl, Aubrey (1983). *Prehistoric Astronomy and Ritual.* Aylesbury, Bucks: Shire Archaeology.

Calvin, William H. (2001). *How the Shaman Stole the Moon.* USA: An Authors Guild Backinprint.com edition. (working out the problems of archaeoastronomy from first principles, especially at sites in the USA).

Haagensen, Erling and Lincoln, Henry (2000). *The Templar's Secret Island.* London: Cassell. (Medieval geometric surveying on Bornholm in the Baltic)

Hadingham, Evan (1983). *Early Man and the Cosmos.* London: Heinemann.

Hancock, Graham and Faiia, Santha (1998). *Heaven's Mirror. Quest for the Lost Civilization.* London: Penguin.

Heath, Robin (1998). *Sun, Moon and Stonehenge.* Cardigan, Wales: Bluestone Press.

Heath, Robin and Michell, John (2004). *The Measure of Albion.* Cardigan, Wales: Bluestone Press. (this book concentrates on the related subject of metrology – the development of systems of measurement and units of measure).

Heggie, Douglas C. (1981). *Megalithic Science.* London: Thames and Hudson.

Heggie, Douglas C. (ed.) (1982). *Archaeoastronomy in the Old World.* Cambridge: Cambridge University Press. (a collection of short academic articles)

Krupp, Dr.E.C. (1983). *Echoes of the Ancient Skies. The astronomy of lost civilizations*. Oxford: Oxford University Press.

MacKie, Euan W. (1977). *Science and Society in Prehistoric Britain*. London:Elek.

Magli, Giulio (English edn. 2009). *Mysteries and Discoveries of Archaeoastronomy. From Giza to Easter Island*. New York: Copernicus Books.

North, John. (1996). *Stonehenge: A New Interpretation of Prehistoric Man and the Cosmos*. New York: The Free Press. (not just on Stonehenge, despite its title!)

Santillana, Giorgio de and Dechend, Hertha von (1969). *Hamlet's Mill*. Boston, USA: Godine. (Difficult but hugely influential book about astronomy and myth)

Temple, Robert (1999). *The Crystal Sun*. London: Arrow. (A fascinating book arguing that glass lenses may have been used in prehistory).

Wood, John Edwin (1978). *Sun, Moon and Standing Stones*. Oxford: Oxford University Press. (a good basic textbook)

Some background books on archaeology:

Hayman, Richard (1997). *Riddles in Stone. Myths, Archaeology and the Ancient Britons*. London: The Hambledon Press.

Johnson, Matthew (1999). *Archaeological Theory. An Introduction*. Oxford: Blackwell.

Russell, Miles (2002). *Monuments of the British Neolithic*. Stroud, Gloucestershire: Tempus.

Some useful books on individual sites and countries:

Aveni, Anthony F. (2001). *Skywatchers. Revised version of Skywatchers of Ancient Mexico*. Austin, Texas: University of Texas Press.

Fell, Barry (1989). *America BC*. New York: Pocket Books.

Freeman, Gordon R. (2009). *Canada's Stonehenge*. Canada: Kingsley Publishing.

Heath, Robin (2010). *Bluestone Magic. A Guide to the Prehistoric Monuments of West Wales*. Cardigan, Wales: Bluestone Press.

Hoskin, Michael (2001). *Tombs, Temples and their Orientations. A New Perspective on Mediterranean Prehistory*. Bognor Regis: Ocarina Books.

O'Kelly, Michael J. (1982). *Newgrange. Archaeology, art and legend*. London: Thames and Hudson.

Mann, Nicholas R. & Glasson, Philippa (2007). *The Star Temple of Avalon. Glastonbury's Ancient Observatory Revealed*. Wells, Somerset: The Temple Publications.

Patton, Mark; Rodwell, Warwick and Finch, Olga (1999). *La Hougue Bie. Jersey*. Jersey: Societe Jersiaise.

Ponting, Gerald and Ponting, Margaret (2000). *New Light on the Stones of Callanish*. Stornaway: G & M Ponting.

Ruggles, Clive (1999). *Astronomy in Prehistoric Britain and Ireland*. New Haven and London: Yale University Press.

Some background books on astronomy:

Evans, James (1998). *The History and Practice of Ancient Astronomy*. New York and Oxford: Oxford University Press. (Largely about ancient Greek astronomy from about 700 BCE).

Heath, Robin (1999 & 2006). *Sun, Moon and Earth*. Glastonbury: Wooden Books.

Hoskin, Michael (ed.) (1999). *The Cambridge Concise History of Astronomy*. Cambridge: Cambridge University Press.

North, John (1994). *The Fontana History of Astronomy and Cosmology*. London: Fontana Press.

Walker, C. (ed) (1996). *Astronomy Before the Telescope*. London: British Museum Press.

Books on Stonehenge:

(You could form a small library of books on this one site alone!)

Burl, Aubrey (2007). *A Brief History of Stonehenge*. London: Robinson.

Chippindale, Christopher (2004). *Stonehenge Complete*. London: Thames and Hudson.

Hawkins, Gerald S. (1966). *Stonehenge Decoded*. Glasgow: Fontana/Collins.

Heath, Robin (1993). *A Key to Stonehenge*. Cardigan, Wales: Bluestone Press.

Heath, Robin (2000). *Stonehenge*. Powys, Wales: Wooden Books.

History of Archaeoastronomy:

Lockyer, Norman (1906). *Stonehenge and other British Stone Monuments Astronomically Considered.* London: Macmillan. (reprinted by Kessinger Publishing).

Lockyer, Norman. *Dawn of Astronomy*. (reprinted by Kessinger Publishing)

Michell, John (2001). *A Little History of Astro-Archaeology*. New York: Thames and Hudson. (an excellent introduction)

Newham, C.A. (1967). *The Astronomical Significance of Stonehenge*. Moon Publications.

Thom, Alexander (1967). *Megalithic Sites in Britain.* Oxford: Oxford University Press. (Professor Thom's demanding books are now rare editions, but anyone seriously interested in archaeoastronomy soon wants to possess them!)

Thom, Alexander (1971). *Megalithic Lunar Observatories.* Oxford: Oxford University Press.

Thom, A. and Thom, A.S. (1978). *Megalithic Remains in Britain and Brittany.* Oxford: Clarendon Press.

Ancient Seafaring and Exploration:
Evidence for ancient seafaring and navigation supports the idea that people in prehistory had a close knowledge of the skies.

Cunliffe, Barry (2001). *The Extraordinary Voyage of Pytheas the Greek*. New York: Walker and Company.

Cunliffe, Barry (2001). *Facing the Ocean. The Atlantic and its Peoples*. Oxford: Oxford University Press.

Heyerdahl, Thor (1950). *The Kon-Tiki Expedition*. London: Allen & Unwin.
(Gripping real-life adventure story – followed by others equally exciting)

Heyerdahl, Thor (1978). *Early Man and the Ocean. The beginning of navigation and seaborn civilisations*. London: Allen and Unwin. (a general and academic approach to the subject).

Lewis, David (1972). *We The Navigators. The Ancient Art of Landfinding in the Pacific*. Honolulu: University Press of Hawaii.

Zapp, Ivar and Erikson, George (1998). *Atlantis in America. Navigators of the Ancient World*. Adventures Unlimited Press: Illinois, USA.

Websites: (just a few to get started)

The Megalithic Portal – world-wide ancient site database. Thousands of photographs. Grid references and co-ordinates of sites given. Forum for exchange of ideas.
www.megalithic.co.uk

The Modern Antiquarian – massive resource for news, information and images of ancient sites across Europe. Forums and blogs.
www.themodernantiquarian.com

Megalithic Studies mid-Wales
(impressive site with descriptions of selected places around the world with their astronomical alignments, as well as useful explanatory pages on astronomical concepts)
www.megalithicsites.co.uk

Royal Commission websites:

on the Ancient and Historical Monuments of Scotland
www.rcahms.gov.uk

on the Ancient and Historical Monuments of Wales
www.rcahmw.gov.uk

on the Ancient and Historical Monuments of England
(merged with English Heritage 1999)
www.buildingconservation.com

Look out also for photographers' websites designed to provide information on sunlight and moonlight at particular places and times.

Apps for i phones may also contain useful measurement converters and other relevant information.

Leicester University website for GetDec:
http://www.le.ac.uk/archaeology/rug/aa/progs/getdec.html

Transverse Mercator Calculator for use with GetDec:
http://www.dmap.co.uk/ll2tm.htm

Index Sky and Landscape

The
Countryside Code

Be safe, plan ahead and follow any signs.

Check weather conditions in advance and let someone
know where you are going and when you expect to return.

Avoid crops and leave gates and property as you find them.

Protect plants and animals and take your litter home.

Take care not to start fires accidentally in dry weather.

Consider other people. For example, don't block field
gateways with your vehicle.

Notes

For more details of methods,
books and research see

www.skyandlandscape.com

Front cover picture based on **Le Grand dolmen du Ferussac,
France (Lat: 43.8 N Long: 3.5 E)**

Back cover picture summer solstice sunset at the
Blaenglasffrwd Cairn, Mid Wales